THE COMING-DOWN TIME

THE COMING-DOWN TIME

ROBERT SELBY

[signature]

Shoestring Press

Printed by imprintdigital
Upton Pyne, Exeter
www.digital.imprint.co.uk

Typesetting by narrator
www.narrator.me.uk
info@narrator.me.uk
033 022 300 39

Published by Shoestring Press
19 Devonshire Avenue, Beeston, Nottingham, NG9 1BS
(0115) 925 1827
www.shoestringpress.co.uk

First published 2020
© Copyright: Robert Selby
© Cover image: 'Planting Trees' by Clare Leighton, courtesy of
the estate of Clare Leighton

The moral right of the author has been asserted.

ISBN 978-1-912524-51-8

ACKNOWLEDGEMENTS

Acknowledgements are due to the following publications in which some of these poems have previously appeared: *Agenda, Ambit, Areté, Caught by the River, Days of Roses I* and *II, Exegesis, The High Window, The London Magazine, The Manhattan Review, New Statesman, PN Review, Poetry Birmingham, Smoke, The Spectator, Structo, Times Literary Supplement.*

Five poems appeared as No. 19 in Clutag Press's *Five Poems* pamphlet series.

Special thanks are due to Jennifer Edgecombe, Declan Ryan, John Fuller, Andrew McNeillie, Andrew Motion, John Lucas, André Naffis-Sahely, and Malene Engelund.

CONTENTS

I EAST OF IPSWICH

II SHADOWS ON THE BARLEY

III   CHEVENING

I

East of Ipswich

i.m.
George Gissing 1919–2007
and
Lea Gissing 1923–2006

'I like this ol' country best. Suffolk.'
'Your roots are deep deep, Oliver?'
'Yeah, I like ol' Suffolk. I don't think you can beat it, do you?'
'Oh, I don't think so. I think there's worse places to be, don't you?'
'Yeah, 'course there is … deserts and all that, y'don't want to go there, do you?'

– AKENFIELD, 1974 film adaptation

The Gardiner had the Souldier's place,
And his more gentle Forts did trace;
The Nursery of all things green
Was then the only Magazeen;
The Winter Quarters were the Stoves,
Where he the tender Plants removes.
But War all this doth overgrow:
We Ord'nance Plant, and Powder sow.

– ANDREW MARVELL

I   IN GOD'S PREVENIENT GRACE

He came from a long line of men who worked
now-extinct equine trades: wheelwright, ostler,
coachman, horseman. His groom father begat
nine in the 'coming-down time'. They were Chapel.

The redbrick Methodists, owning no graveyard,
are permitted to join the heaped-up past
among St Bartholomew's windswept grass
during a terse, wind-scattered prayer.

He left two-dozen books, one a schoolboy
adventure story: *Every Inch a Briton.*
Its cover: a boy in bowtie, waistcoat,
plus-fours, raising his straw boater.

Inside, inscribed by his Sunday school teacher,
dated January 1934,
Ecclesiastes 12:1: *Remember*
now thy Creator in the days of thy youth.

II   ORFORD

He grew up beside
Europe's largest vegetated shingle spit.
Across it, North Sea winds bring word of mermen
and invasion. MOD buildings stand disused on the peninsula,

softened by time
in the hearts of the locals, who call them
pagodas. In the war, a friendly destroyer some miles
off-shore mistook the village for the nearby firing range

of Sudbourne Battle,
shelling the road he was born and raised in.
The special constable rang up the Navy and asked
please would they kindly cease fire. No one was lost.

Like much of old
England now, it stars in colour supplements:
the Crown & Castle has become a high-end hotel
and restaurant owned by a TV personality, the tamed ness

a Grade One Site
of Special Scientific Interest. But weak glows
in night windows still hint at a hearth-comfort, stolen
against the undying winds that buffet the grassy tombs

of the long-quashed kings
of the East Angles; against the fen demons
that, retold by flame, may burst over the threshold,
into the real. That expressed before King George II's visit

still rings true as the church
bells' peal: 'If the King ask "who are you then?"
we humbly answer: "Orford Men". Who else dare ask,
we answer bluff: "We're Orford Men, and that's enough."'

III   THE END OF THE HORSE AGE

With history yet to give him a greater role,
he cycles many dawn miles
to work the big estates.

Lunchtime he returns for rabbit,
suet pudding; then,
draining his water in a doorway's fallow light,
with no risk of calories dawdling to fat,
he sets out again. And so on, every day.

        The beasts he clicks his tongue at
                    pedalling past
        are Suffolk Punch, built to last:
                    chestnut heavies with names like 'Pegasus',
        bred to lack fetlock feathers
                    (fine on a brewer's or a milkman's dray
        but glue for clods in the field).
                    Gods of the plough they are,
        good doers seventeen hands high
                    with a rump 'like a farm wife's arse'
        and 'the eyes of a Christian'.

Behind him as he pedals on,
his white twill shirt too sweat-stuck to billow,
the gods turn and face the final furrow.

Later, coasting wearily home in the gloaming,
he sees an unblinkered beast
braying smoke in the top field, light
from its side-lamps shining off makers' plates
cast from melted-down horse brasses.

IV ELYSIUM

Away? The next village, the next set of fields.
Only conscription could put him on a train:
when it pulled into the tunnel, the torn world

was immense; when it emerged, the sudden,
blinding light of peace waned to a smaller world
stitched by jets. He returned to the hearth

having seen nothing to allay his suspicions.
His wife would've liked to travel, but it was he
learnt to drive, buying from a local character,

an aged spinster, a rose-taupe Morris Minor,
its protuberant hubcaps recalling
the shallow-crowned kettle or Brodie helmets

still ploughed-up in Flanders, northern France.
When grandchildren return from holiday
with miniature bagpipes that—squeezed—

play a puny 'Scotland the Brave',
she asks: 'What's the time difference in Scotland?'
To spare them, one grandson's planned move

to Tasmania is kept from them
as long as possible.
Before the secret can become untenable,

they, who knew the end of the horse age,
have made their own longest journey,
into the next life, the next set of fields.

V   WHEN THAT WHICH IS PERFECT IS COME

He married Doll in Orford. Lea,
her real name, was shed like the mixed tears
and confetti on the waving platform.
They sat back hand-in-hand and wove away
from the ness, crossing the Stour
to Kent, the terrace house she was born in,
grew up in. There they lived together
seven decades, until death took them
within a tell-tale short time of each other.

Her maiden name, the name
of the most famous Kentish beer hop,
was gone; so too, eventually, were the hops,
the green rows blackening with *Verticulum
Wilt*, one-by-one, until the kells cooled.

VI VISITING DAY

Lightly tapping on the gloss-blue backdoor
with knuckle or car-key, my mother
says 'coo-ee!' (A 'come here' bush-call
Tommy heard Digger use in the Dardanelles

from across death's peninsula, evacuated home
and patched-up parish-proper to mean:
'It's only me, so don't start;
I've let myself in to meet you at your hearth.')

Inside, water on the gas, simmering gently.
The clock correct on its long-life battery.
From his low armchair by the partition
he shakes my hand, as if I'm a man.

His hands dwarf mine.
I already know this won't change with time.
Suffolk reserve in his 'Hello
Robert': words are weeds that don't fall to the hoe.

Wet-cheeked from my grandmother's kiss,
I take the chair by the window where Moggie sits.
No. 15's tortoiseshell, she'll materialise
in the shed's shadow as two neon eyes,

alley-tense to reclaim her throne.
All the while muttering about her rightful home,
grandma will place out a saucer
of full-cream milk on the back step for her.

VII   THE DIVIDE

They're in the kitchen, the one place well-infused
with natural light, built to extend home
into a century already

nonagenarian. My grandmother,
making jelly for the trifle, disappears
in the kettle's steam. His brace-clips gleam;

his checked shirt, unbuttoned, reveals white vines
thriving in his vest's trelliswork. Sleeves rolled up:
after a lifetime outside in whatever

Mother Nature throws, it's less of a leap
to come home and peel potatoes than for
the suited man who steps off the evening train.

Tea is served in glass cups too hot to hold.
He stirs two sugars into mine, three into his own—
making up for all the sugar boats that went down.

She hasn't skimped on the milk, full-cream stuff
delivered in pint bottles with silver foil crowns
by the white-coated Unigate milkman

dawn brings whistling from his three-wheeled float.
He whistles under our windows too,
but clinkingly leaves pints crowned red and white:

semi-skimmed. This says we're a household
that cannot thin calories from full-cream milk
into olive-skinned gauntness, into a handshake

formidable beneath piercing eyes in deep sockets.
My father, after all, is one of the suited men
who'll step off the evening train.

I wait for grandma to cross to the oak dresser
and liberate the McVitie's chocolate biscuits.
But she's back there, busy with the whisk.

And he's back further, in my mother's memory,
straining elderflower through muslin
into the tin bath, turning light into wine.

VIII   WE MAY ALLOW OURSELVES A BRIEF PERIOD OF REJOICING

Their table couldn't accommodate us all
when my brothers were also there: he'd eat
from a tray across his knees, in his armchair
next to the gas fire and the record player
that, later, became a CD player.

After the doctor told him 'things aren't exactly
one hundred per cent the way we'd like them to be',
when canned water became heavy,
an outside tap went in so he could hose his beds
with still-judicious rain.

To drown-out the drilling
he sat in the armchair with headphones on
listening to remastered big band and swing,
black-and-white characters in victory rolls
or pomade, singing him back

to that walk up the garden path
when he was blind to the barren beds,
kitbag over one shoulder,
about to press play on a paused life,
a spit-and-polished husband returning to his wife.

IX   TEAM PHOTO

Never used in the day, the front room
was so-called as a door—always mysterious
beyond a heavy blackout curtain—admitted post.

A net curtain stirred and blinked with traffic
passing feet away. The room contained:
a TV with fake wood trim, aerial aimed

at the gas fireplace, over which five shelves
housed photos, framed, of five grandchildren;
a tile-topped coffee table made in the Seventies

by a son-in-law, a frosted fruit bowl on top;
a battleship grey rotary-dial telephone,
emergencies-only use; a brown, prickly sofa.

       Presiding over it all,
keeping unmellowed a wide rectangle of wall,
a black and white regimental photograph:

hundreds upon hundreds of men in tiered rows,
each with the same field service caps, squints
and noonday shadows under the nose,

but he not one.
There was a story, lost, as to why.
Doubtful it was down to superstition,

a fear the lens would steal his soul.
More prosaic: he was on garrison duty—
organising mail home, or setting up the goal.

X HELLFIRE CORNER

The sun had burned mist off the hills,
revealing German POWs at their ploughs.
Spring's breeze silvered the birches
burgeoning greenly behind The Duke's Head.
He was at the bus stop with Doll

when the V-bomb came over, its low growl
forged deep within Hell's foundry.
Then it stopped. Silence.
The hedge birds, the linnets and larks, stopped.
Spring's breeze darkened to a draught.

He pulled her down, throwing himself on top of her.
'Any excuse!' we quipped
to lighten her funeral reception—
she a munitions girl
who became a doting wife and mother, and grandmother,

whom he couldn't shield with his body
the final time.

XI   THE BIG GUNS

Memories, like poppies, are stirred by trauma.
At Doll's funeral reception, fragile
red flowers bloomed in a once sunless bed.
The room fell hushed to what he said.

We knew he'd seen action across Europe
after D-Day with the Royal Artillery,
but now were told an enemy gun,
emplaced in a church, was neutralised,

leaving no church. Offered bombardier,
he turned it down to remain one of the lads.
Demobbed, he stowed his Enfield in the attic:
you can take the boy out of the country…

Then came a sixty-year, losing battle
with leg ulcers caused by working on
his big gun. Eligible for recompense,
he filed for nothing,

only from God the narrow peace in which
to see his children and grandchildren grow up,
like miracle marrows to flaunt
at the County Show, however flawed.

XII PERSONAL EFFECTS

A pair of toddler's clogs—
vamps painted with the Dutch tricolour.

A black-and-white, dated *Summer 41*—
him in helmet and puttees, full kit, Enfield at the ready.

A battered leather wallet enclosing—
one near-petrified pressed flower;

one scrap of paper so aptly foxed
as if aged by tea-dipping,

the war a history project.
Scrawled in pencil when he heard it was all over:

May 7th, 1945.
Left camp at 10.30am at Bad Oeynhausen.

Crossed Rhine into Holland at Roermond.
There is a Naafi on the train

(10 cigarettes, 1 chocolate and tea cakes).
4.45am—Arrived at Tournai.

XIII   TOURNAI

He files out under a ceiling of starlight.
The high jinks of the train—they'd smoked,
eaten Yank chocolate, shaved off
one of bombardier's eyebrows as he kipped—
spills into the platform parade.
Sarge receives a bit of backchat.

Something has changed.
It's there, too, in the dawn:
the belfry's white pigeons pouting lazily,
the light dressing the cathedral's wounds
and dappling the path along the Scheldt
suggest a more permanent R&R.

He and the lads head for the Musée
des Beaux-Arts, but the kiss-blowing
of the passing Belgian girls
keeps them on the street, feigning nonchalance:
cap through shoulder-board, hands in pockets,
cig in corner of mouth like Bogart.

They walk Rue Saint-Martin and Chaussée
de Willemeau until they reach the town
cemetery, where they lean or lie on the tombs
next to six hundred British dead
from the last show. He takes a light, lies back,
draws, and breathes out a trail of smoke
into the clear blue sky between the yews.

XIV   DUNTON GREEN

Smoke rises into the clear blue sky
between the yews. His gaze falls
and he sees not the lads among the graves
but a bride, invincibly white
in a dappled crowd—his daughter,
whom he's just given away with dry eyes
veiling the demolition of his heart.

He taps out his pipe against the Morris's wing,
pockets it, and walks back over.
Men ease from the congregation.
'Sunderland are winning' he declares:
two or three move to the transistor
on the passenger seat, only believing it
if they hear it with their own ears.

In the front room, eating finger food
off paper plates, they watch Bobby Stokoe,
Mackems manager, run across Wembley turf
to embrace keeper Jim Montgomery,
whose double save at the death
has secured the biggest shock
in cup final history.

Stokoe's trademark trilby comes off.
His run—arms aloft, hat precarious—
is already passing into bronze,
his tears into rain,
when the newlyweds' Allegro rumbles
in a cloud of exhaust and rattling tin
up the cheering, blossom-moted lane.

XV   SATURDAY MORNING FOOTBALL

The old battle formation: baggage to the rear.
I was hidden in defence. Blood up with boredom,
eager to change minds, I'd foray out, slide in,
and miss. He's still there, on the touchline,
waiting for me to do something to make him proud.
Leaning on the seat-stick pride stops him unfolding—
even now, when the diagnosis is no pulse—
he's a silent figure my nocturnal dog walk
runs aground on. 'It's been twenty years,' I plead,
backing away, lead and all my adulthood loosed.
Dawn finds me muddy-mouthed and prone,
watching through grass-blades their striker slotting it home.

XVI   THE PEACE THAT PASSES HUMAN UNDERSTANDING

I don't visit him in hospital,
preferring my last memory of him to be
the strength in his goodbye handshake
his gauntness belies,

able to think a little while longer
the coil can unwind forever, not end
in the soul's release through the discreet door
in the great walled garden.

XVII   AN IDLE WIND

As he slid behind the curtain
to 'Moonlight Becomes You',
my mother, a girl again,
waved and said: 'Goodbye, Dad.'

Now, in turn, we kneel as at a flowerbed
to unpot his and Doll's intimate grit
together into the sexton's care.
Some blows over us, into our faces, our hair.

> The worst of the weathers to work in, he said,
> rubbing his arms and shaking his head,
> indoors, twenty years after retirement:
> undoes your labours, upsets your stride;

> there'd be nowhere to hide.
> And an idle wind, well, that's the worst
> of all winds: moves right through you
> rather than take the trouble to go round.

My mother likes it, says the dark hollies
whitening in the wind like surf
create a sense of life, as though the dead
are reincarnate as leaves, the very turf.

Out of the corner of my eye, I glimpse him
leaning against the ruined Norman chancel,
his young face weakly lit
by the struck match he's holding to his pipe:

collar up, flat-cap down, all skulky-like,
for he's in the out-of-bounds garage among
tennis racquets and limousines, sheltering
from an idle wind and the Lordship's gaze.

XVIII   THE DAYLIGHT

Leaving the mason with his cement gun
to glue down the desk-style headstone,
we enter the church. The door thuds shut.

A musty silence but for our footsteps,
the immortal draught in the tie-beamed roof
harrying the candles we light,

the harried light setting the font's lions
and wildmen dancing. Along the south wall,
the Great War memorial bears more names

than Orford has roofs, a congregation
that would cram the pews long since ripped out,
replaced by Victorian schoolroom chairs

with little bible-holders on their backs.
We go among them, admiring the knitted
hassocks depicting local landmarks, crests:

the WI, Methodist church, Scout group;
the houses in the road he grew up in,
the road shelled by friendly fire.

We're given the all-clear. Against the wind
we arrange favourites in the inkwell
to soften the newness of the sandstone:

pink tulips, white narcissi, purple speedwell.
We take photos, then all cram in for one:
a family with two members un-there.

Divining the smokehouse by its smoke,
one of us buys eels;
we watch the fish boats and tugs clank

against their moorings on the glittering ness.
Time, and a long pilgrimage, narrows
the daylight between mourner and tourist.

I drive home nervously from the ness
the blue Vauxhall Corsa
he exchanged his rusted Morris for.
My brother beside me navigates,
hand near the handbrake, poised for scrapes.

Past pine forest concealing
an old Air Force base gone to weed,
past farm hardware piled in disused quarry pits,
past salt marsh invading heath, slinking back out,
and a tractor's arm trimming a hedgerow,

the lane grows congested:
a spoonbill has been spotted on Havergate Island.
Some observers believe it the same bird
seen last week at the mouth of the River Humber.
Others detect minute plumage differences.

Men in camouflage unpack tripods from car boots.
On local radio a Suffolk Police spokesman says:
'We have managed to send a message out
to the twitcher community
asking them to park more considerately.'

      Home,
          relieved,
                my brother goes for a lie down.
He's woken by our mother's scream.
Looking out the kitchen window, she'd seen
a flat-capped old man re-parking the Corsa.
It was my father: she thought she'd seen hers.

XX WILF

He left us Wilf, a barefoot, knee-high stone rustic.
A battered old boater, waistcoat, neckerchief
keep him decent in the flowerbed he hogs,
sat on a stone bench with his stone lunch
wrapped in newspaper beside him.

Unflapped by the Union Jack once struck
above his head to mark Remembrance Sundays,
St George's Days and royal anniversaries,
he has lunched in a century's lees.

He's weathered white, locked in old age
like Tithonus: denied the eternal sleep.
In fact, rounded-off by rain, his feet balling
into boots, he could be growing younger.

Now Lordship of my parents' flowerbed,
he watches with hard eyes a Worcester
Pearmain apple tree come into fruit,
thrushes loot the rowan of red berries,
the day's shadow move about the dial.

II

Shadows on the Barley

...your large speeches may your deeds approve,
That good effects may spring from words of love.

– KING LEAR

THE WINTER WOOD

How easily people forget things,
 the winter wood displays.
Hanging in tangles limp from brambles
 are scarves that were gifts on Christmas Day,
and gloves adorn waymarkers and fences
 like cairns, or the butcher-bird's prey.
Now and then, a neatly folded Barbour
 or pair of hiking boots, as if a rambler,

wishing to ramble no more, drowned himself
 in the river down by the cattle byre;
had to wait until a full day and night
 of rain, until it could swell no higher;
thrust field guide in tweed one last time,
 hung binoculars from wind-bent brier,
and swanned in between dripping pine
 up to his deer-stalker—the only sign

a man gulped hard in there, ending things
 as easily as people forget things. Frost
stiffens body and bower just the same,
 and all the walkers' accessories lost
from their selves soften in squally rain,
 decay, forming a rag-and-bone copse
with knitted limbs of knotted fabric
 standing testament to the losing habit.

UPON THE ALTAR LAID

Left over from a sovereign's entry into
nonagenarianism, Union Jack
bunting flicks in a light easterly, this evening
before men move one hundred years ago
forward into the unbarbed ground between us.
Those pallid faces, smiling in black and white,
lifting a fork of bully, or hand blurred,
moving away a smoke—

                someone's cleaned them,
coloured them, so that all distance pales:
their eyes' blue; their vests' eggshell blue;
a tunic's second button blacked, for fallen
kin; a Signals rider's sky-blue armband;
blue Overseas Service Chevrons above
a hand cupping the billet-farm's liver and white
spaniel pup; the farm-girl's red hair, green shawl;
the socks pegged-out, baby blue to royal;
the scarlet puggarees on the Kiwis' lemon-
squeezer hats. The red of the red crosses.

          ~To Lieutenant Butterworth G.S.K., MC~
          You set Housman
and Sussex folksongs to music, on war's eve
saw your banks of green willow and joined
the Durham miners; led them to take the wood
at Pozières, and, before you could receive
your MC, fell holding Munster Alley.
Buried hastily under fire, unrecovered,
Thiepval has your name, your Green Willow
forms-up redcoats for the slow inspection.
          George, it was the Somme.

Your father William ('warehouseman')
married your mother Johanna ('confectioner')
at St Saviour's, Southwark, on Boxing Day
1887. Including two
still-born, they bore thirteen. You, the sixth,
came 1897. We thus intuit
before reading on: you served. You joined
the 8th Battalion, London Regiment—
the Post Office Rifles—and at 1345 hours
on Saturday 7th October 1916
your Stamp-Lickers went over the top
in an advance on the Grid Line
below the Butte de Warlencourt.

> *The creeping barrage was only inter-*
> *-mittently effective and the inexperience*
> *of the new draft showed in a tendency to bunch.*

For her remaining forty years, your mother's
heart was like Thiepval: your name engraved upon it.
Black weeds took root, wouldn't pull,
and stayed, tended. Her maiden name was Spiess.

Henry James Keen, I, your great-grandnephew,
will be pleased to meet you
later, beyond England,
in the intractable white of peace.

~Interlude~
Hunched over the keys, in blue shirt and braces,
your brother Bill's at the piano, playing what?
Another brother, Charlie, DSM
(for gallantry in conveying messages
and attending wounded under heavy fire)
stands poised with the bow's horsehair hovering
above the violin to his neck, waiting
for a way in; while Bertie, nearest you in age,

taps time with his foot and raises the reed
            to his lips, smoky gaslight glinting off brass.
You're there, Jimmy, among the drinkers; sipping,
            elbow on the bar, proud—envious also,
for you can't play, never having got the knack;
            and your brothers can't call on some of your spoof
spoon-percussion because you are dead,

and George, the window over your desk at Radley,
looking onto the playing field, stands open,
letting escape the music that will never be,
admitting the sound of Thomas's larks
        singing as they did
        when we went up in dark and were shelled
        Larks at 5.15 and blackbirds at 6 till it snowed
        or rained at 8
        Frosty and clear and some blackbirds singing
        in the quiet of exhausted battery, everyone
        just having breakfast at 9.30
The curtains, blowing in. The field, darkling.
The skylarks and hedge birds of all the counties
falling silent, one by one.

                    Tomorrow,
in a dawn unbroken by eastern guns,
a flag will down-shiver for men of this district
but not of these times. Come, let us be going
from beneath the green trees.
Strong feelings for this place—are they now
            parochial weed, whimsy's butterfly,
            unabsorbed from foxed books, from hymns and song
            and harassed by the sight of the Somme's
            rows and the only possible question: 'why'?
                    Hard, George, to know
if the feelings the late violin sends through me
are now commonly shared, if they ever were,

and what exactly they are—like England,
still here as a flag, station stops, the Household Division
shouldering arms at the chimes of Big Ben,
cow parsley in the wheat, and the Glorious Dead,
> if that is England. At the end,
> a place to stand beyond,
> like some lambkin, undone.

THE SYCAMORE

'Up the narrow road beside the tea-room
and you pass an iron-eating tree…'
– Gazetteer for Scotland

The black-faced smithy's boy of Brig o'Turk
propped his bicycle against the sycamore
before his final shift at the clanging hearth,
soon to head for war to escape the bore
of pouring coal into the firepot's girth.
Proud of his young apprentice, the old mentor
carted the new recruit home on his last day,
so the bicycle remained in the keep of the tree.

As the smithy's boy made corporal and set sail,
the creeping sycamore began a slow advance.
As bugles sounded from sad shires their lonely scales,
the bicycle was raised on a timber lance.
When the smithy's boy fell at Passchendaele
and the village shuttered in remembrance,
the sycamore drew about the bicycle,
clutching to its bark the spokes and saddle.

Long since the blacksmith sold off the yard,
since war ended, resprouted, withered again,
and the Trossachs became a National Park,
the bicycle protrudes still, a man-made limb
mimicking new growth. The ribbed handlebars
wait for young hands to re-clasp them,
pull free the frame and tour off, roadworthy,
this cast-iron memorial in the skyward lee.

THE GALILEAN MOONS

Io

Often the coastguard is called
out by a distress flare
only to find Jupiter.

The white cows in the black field
could crush a man in the lane,
invade a football field,
make the motorway stand still—
but follow our quad bike
in sleepwalk to night shelter.

Always with Jupiter, cows.
Disguising himself as one,
or turning his victims bovine,
so he goes undenounced.

Europa

Could these beasts swim to Crete?
Indoors their muscle
trots tame as meat
among the hay, iron,
and idle, hanging teat-cups.

Certainly I have seen them sidle
into the Stour and stand,
watching their faces in the water—
as if they can command
the countenance of water.

When the gate is pulled to
they turn and watch you,
eyes the cataracted
marble of Europa.
Black ink in milk.
The moon on the Stour.

Ganymede

The night's getting up,
plucking the poplar trees'
harp of sighs.

Jupiter, the old pederast,
who took a Troy boy
and had him as his catamite,
is aloft again tonight.

Ganymede. Pale grey
crosscut with dark grey:
the Ruhr from the air
below the bomber's moon,
the brilliant craters
blasts or flak-fire.

Moonlight maps the barn's
skeletal eaves,
nullifies the scarecrow
standing for lead thieves.

The night goes slack;
we blow into our gloves;
and then snow.

Callisto

Night-time inside the snow globe.
Flakes fall out of the black
into barn-light across the yard.
No susurrance from poplars.
The motorway is strangled.
The cows steam.

Jupiter, disguised as Diana,
coaxed Callisto to his lair.
Orbits aligned, sped and tightened.
She became a bear,
pregnant and frightened,
setting among the stars,
a moon without resonance
renouncing Jupiter's dominance—
she wears the scars.

Night-time inside the snow globe.
Flakes fall out of the black,
hiding Jupiter and the stars.
You lean back on me, snow-gazing,
wanting snow on your face,
on your spectacles.
I taste the snow in your hair.

DEAR RALPH CROZIER

The Weald below was white as a burial shroud.
I waited for my taxi to fight its way off,
then opened the pre-Reformation oak door.

The hush within almost matched the one without.
Two hundred mourners, and none looked around:
they were nearly all your flock, Ralph.

The vicar signed your eulogy with the arms
of a railing minister, but the countenance
of a calm faith. Hands spoke silent psalms.

Under the vaults, my mind was a shedding bough,
lightening at the fall of each good word,
interpreted from the transept. Sorry Ralph:

conscious of others with hearing, I only
mumbled the Lord's Prayer, but we were friends
because my life so differed from yours,

mention of which over chess was strictly
'verboten', till brandy loosened your tongue
and you'd say how you'd only just begun.

Under the vaults, hemmed tight, in winter wear,
I smiled at an old expression of yours:
'Hot as a blackbird nesting in a traffic light.'

Relief: you were borne down the shining nave
into snowlight, a silence broken
by processional heels on the gritted steps.

Ralph, the diminuendo of startled birds
recalled our walks on clear days, while you
still could, in the grounds of your life's work.

AN AURELIAN WATCHES HIS WIFE

'Behind each great naturalist of the period,
there was a wife.'
 – R.V. Welch, *Butterflies & Seashells: The Victorian Naturalists*

How can that snow-lit neck of yours be purpled
so it leads justice to his skewed door?
You hold your hem up as you scatter grain
about the coop. All is glaring on this white plane:

from outside the dim depths of his warped shed
I caught your whispered promises
like the specimens we netted together last summer—
with held breath and soft tread. I pin them to the page:

'For him I'm a nag,
but for you my love
I'm a trotting-horse
bristling for your thighs'—
'He'll be left to keep house—'
'—with those mild hands—'
'—while mine glide
with dexterity
between your—'
'—above a beech-screened
eloper's inn—'
'—for a sovereign
no one'll bother us therein—'

No, I won't get by with a talent only
for what makes Society heads nod approvingly
over their fireside port, lacking housekeeper
and cook since you wished this place 'just for ourselves'.

But out there, you said, demands plotting,
the persuasion of an earthy literacy,
and the scholar we chose—well, you did–
is like the caterpillar of the Large Blue,

leaping dead-eye from his thyme leaf into
my credulousness; we the callow ants,
taking him in, fattening him up as one
of our wintering own. When these short days thaw

he'll burst out—with you.
Now you look around, and see me, and smile
redly, as if desiring to re-ignite
new love's weakness for begrimed beauty.

But I'm no just-born mayfly,
urgent on his first and final day:
you want he who chops firewood in the copse.
I can hear him at it, stripped to his shirt

despite the cold, his brace-clips shining
in the last sunlight, glittering to old gold.
So can you. Grain sticks to your palms:
with every chop, you picture him bending

to balance another block, then straighten,
his colt breath silver in the under-trees.
A glinting arc, the fall true, the silence split.
You move inside, breathless in your burn

for his beastliness to swell, befit your crime,
unsuspecting on your return
me slipped from credulity's chrysalis,
these mild hands possessed of a length of twine.

ACTING

I am Captain Phoebus de Châteaupers—
    without a ride, granted, but the budget
        stretched to false whiskers, red cape, breastplate,
           and I can deliver 'Halt, scoundrels, let
                the girl go!' as well as any, when on I rush,

leading the counterwatch from the front,
    and clutch Esmeralda to me as they
        pile in with quarterstaves. Over her shoulder
           I can just make out faces in the rows
                nearest the stage, including yours.

Did I, knight in shining (plastic) armour,
    thrill you with my gallant entry? Did it
        portray me in a whole new light, dashing,
           in the nick of time, before the footlights?
                Did my chivalrous act cleave your defences,

pierce your stubborn heart like a lance point?
    As I pause, regaining breath, ready for
        Esmeralda to turn to me, and thank me,
           and want her leave, then become smitten,
                hypnotised forever by my handsome face,

do you imagine yourself in her place,
    and begin to reassess your choice,
        a choice your presence here suggests is not
           irreversible? In two days you fly
                to Hong Kong to be with a dying uncle,

yet take time out to watch me badly act.
    The fracas nears its end. Please, meet my eye
        and, with yours, tell me I did not mistake
           the setting sun for our aurora,
                that snow-lit afternoon in the long ground

when you befriended a chestnut horse
and, stroking his blaze, named him after me.
That when you are in Sham Shui Po,
taking respite from your vigil, downtown
among the fabric stalls and computer arcades,

it will be me you call. Can I discern that,
from your expression in the half-dark?
But here's my cue, my name is asked:
'Captain Phoebus de Châteaupers, my dear.
At your service.'

BRUNSWICK, MAINE

*'It is estimated that fewer than a half-dozen of the public parking spaces
will be lost due to the placement of the statue.'*
– Town Council minutes

Joshua Chamberlain stands in the square
in his double-breasted high bronze jacket,
high bronze face showing a decade of wear,
the frost-bitten favourite of Brunswick,
Union general, cap in hand—in the thick of it.
The piebald and downright dirty snow
adorns the old house of Harriet Beecher Stowe,

author of *Uncle Tom's Cabin*. This is Maine
on the Androscoggin, the Pine Tree State,
so snow blows in off the Appalachian range,
sweeping over the ice sheets of Sebago Lake
into the mouth of the Atlantic's roll and wake.
North Pole photos by Peary and Macmillan,
Inuit artefacts, shiver in the Arctic Museum.

Meantime, we're outside the hardware store
lagged up fierce in muff and windcheater,
squeezing a radiator and some two-by-four
into the trunk of our snow-covered Toyota.
A flatpack cot on the back seat teeters
as we crawl our homeward escape,
passing ghosts of upturned boats round the cape.

Joshua Chamberlain stands in the square
in his double-breasted high bronze jacket,
cold promontory without the least fanfare,
solemn, pious embodiment of Brunswick,
watching the snow come on fast now, come on thick,
whiten the piebald and mask our exit tracks;
conceal the old town from all but old maps.

BURNING THE CLOCKS

My train slows into the same old town:
the illumined copper spire of St Mary's church;
the bronze warrior's sodium-lit vigil

above civic pride's floral roundabout,
not in bloom now; in fairy-light bloom
the hornbeams on the high common.

Ten years from having held you
I sit on this train reading online
what you did ten minutes ago,

seeing how a lamp in your sea-view room
cast a sheen on your white, ring-stained
coffee table just this afternoon;

your tabby curled up on a wicker chair;
a fir twig standing in a jam jar—
your Christmas tree;

arrangements you've made with a friend
on where to meet for drinks
before Burning the Clocks.

In the SU bar's light
you were without origin.
For one night talking through smoke with you

the price was an ensorcellment
years beyond our last hug in mortarboards.
My goodness you were nice:

a tide over shingle in your voice,
gull feathers and shells around your neck
as you espoused a seaside city

with all the fervour of someone not of it.
Your real home was a commuter town
where framed photos crowd upright pianos

and birds flute from privets
potteringly kept in cul-de-sacs
nowhere near the sea.

The train each night returns me to mine.
Avoiding that fate, you walk the promenade
of your dreams. It's been a long time.

THE LAND GIRL'S STORY

I

'God speed the plough and the woman who drives it'
  the poster said, and I saw the sun coming up
on a furrow without sock-knitting, without
   ballrooms of platitudes and no partners.
Wearing breeches and gaiters scandalised
  my allotted district, but I won them round
by tanning the hue of their thankless earth.
  My thighs' new muscles moved me to
the village's tolling metronome.
   I wished to be seduced by its old gods.
I remember. All down the lane, snowdrops.
   Nearly lambing time and penitential ashes.
A hand beat mine to the lychgate latch.
   'Allow me,' he stammered—this boy in uniform.

II

I'd been led to believe that church was balm
  for the quaint folk, but I got to going.
The rector did his best. Most were Chapel,
  and not really that: they lowered their voices
in the square so as not to bait the curse
  of the hanged merman; launched rafts of candlelight
each ninth moon for salting sprites to mate by.
  I looked over to the boy in uniform,
the only boy, deep in a darkness pierced
  by stained sunbeams. For the hymns he stood
but didn't sing, one side of his face twitching.
  His officer's coat had the pips missing.
It stayed buttoned-up tight. At the end,
  he replaced his cap in the morning light.

III

'That's Blakewell's boy. Gallipoli.'
He was helping with the hedges when next
I saw him, doing Blakewell's boundary.
I was ploughing with Judd, the horseman. A bully.
The best of his team had been sent to France;
he was left with the nags, beat them for it.
Lead horse was Giant, one no longer—
a show-winner's ghost, marred with tumours.
At the furrow's end he saw the hedge moving
and stopped, crowding the horses behind.
They trampled the plough and our recent pains.
I couldn't pull him on. Judd came roaring,
whipping Giant's head over and over.
He tried backing away, but tangled in the chains.

IV

Judd kicked the lump on Giant's leg.
It tore. The scream! Ice water across you.
It woke me. I was on Judd then, hitting him,
raging into his stinking, beery face.
My curses when he threw me off, and his,
I shan't repeat. He raised the whip to me.
I tripped on the chains and fell,
but the whip never fell. It was Judd screaming
now, and I looked. There was Blakewell's boy,
crouched over him, a cornered fox panting,
throwing his fists into Judd's sides
until the screaming stopped.
He stared back at me then. His face pulsed.
I saw in exhausted eyes a hot, Turkish sun.

V

They found him in the belfry.
   They said he'd go up there when a lad
to see as far as Capel St Andrew,
      Ipswich beyond. On a clear day, the world.
One year he'd etched his name with that
      of his Ella. There was an envelope
of feathers, a farmers' almanack curled by age.
   He'd gone up there to remember
the times they collected feathers together,
      the times he'd study his books up there
alone, after the consumption took her.
   He'd gone and done it there, at the village's
draughty heart, in his lieutenant's coat,
      a pile of hassocks kicked away.

WILD CHERRY

The day came when the wind chose to kill it.
The reach of its roots, stymied by border wall,
was no match for the air's violence.

But you came from the garage with old rope
and lashed the tree by its waist to hope:
a post you hammered badly into grass.

And your look said: 'This wind shan't cast
our spring's white signalman, our summer shade,
into the memory of a tree only,

a surprise sky when looking up from the page;
we shall keep it this-wise for as long
as we're here, my love, and after we've gone

down to intimate compost.
The future unborn wouldn't know what we'd lost,
but they'll enjoy what we have heaved

on this rope like sailors to keep standing
in the gale, will tread its red fallen leaves
and drink, in summer lemonades,

the light it dapples down. We will not fail.'
No, we couldn't let that tree fall, and didn't.
We hear others succumb to chainsaws

across the way, make room for parking,
and the surgeons over-employed each winter
husband for a neatness we call meddling.

Though our cherry leans, rod-straight new boughs
shoot skyward in corrective pursuit
to self-sustain its standing, make its anchor moot.

You follow its progress from your desk,
your eyes blossoming each time the wind rises,
you look up, and it's still there.

THE FIRECRESTS

I

The hazel is ablaze with catkins.
The elms nod their heads in a blue realm.
Below, daffodils kiss down the knoll
to the kissing gate, the brown field beyond
exact, freshly tidied by plough.

You are standing in it,
your face turned up to the new sun,
the tartan scarf—Clan Barclay? The
irrepressible Quakers of Aberdeenshire?—
so yellow around you
on its last outing for,
fingers crossed, more than a wee while.

II

You think you saw firecrests in the elms
so why don't we go and see?
I follow, and my delight
at having you with me
I mask as a possible sighting.

When you lean in to borrow my sightline
up my outstretched arm and finger
the weight against my shoulder
is one of a possible future,
balanced precariously
as a sweet wrapper snagged in a tree.

III

Even here has a coffee franchise.
You sip from a mug
held in both hands
while I look anywhere but into your eyes.
Steam rises to mock-Tudor beams.
The light of afternoon and the smell of beans.
Your legs are pointed toward me,
which I read somewhere means you like me,
or don't, I can't remember.

I shake a sachet of sugar,
as if wisdom might talk from within.
How do I get beyond birds and coffee?
How do I tell you I know you were ill,
I've seen a photo of you
when you were stick-thin?

YOUR BRIGHT JAYS

Darling, all the years left to me wouldn't allow
enough time to describe how much I miss you.
I wanted to tell you I know you're gone now.
I address this not to your imposter, who,
in heart-stopping moments, registers recognition in her eyes—
when I arrive in the cardie you knitted during a knitting phase,
or she slaps my wrist when I slurp my tea, a habit you despised.
But then the sun goes in and her eyes glaze.

I love you, so I visit her every day.
When she won, I had to give you up; I couldn't manage the fear.
She calls after me, frightened, when I come away.
Sometimes it's not my name. Or it is, but with a sneer.
Today, after she was settled, I came home to the kitchen table,
        and cried.
It was so quiet, I could hear your bright jays playing on the roof.
I knew then that you had died.
The body is negotiable fact, the spirit truth.

EXTERIOR WITH A YOUNG WOMAN UPSET

I

Our coming together was a fractious fate:
me always punctual, you always late.
'I can't help it,' you once said, close to tears.

I never understood how you couldn't,
least of all that day your lateness robbed me
of my best-laid plans in plain sight on the street.

Anger convinced me there were others more
appreciative I'd rather meet,
anger that ended the moment you emerged

smiling among the draughty Tube crowd
and on tiptoe I waved,
spoke your name aloud.

II

Our lips landed as close as ambiguity allowed.
You'd come all the way from Ealing for me
when you didn't have to. I see that now.

We entered the Royal Academy to view
Hammershøi's low-key interiors,
his wife, Ida, always with her back to him,

he inspired to capture her nape's grace;
no risk of an Orpheus moment, their love
having passed need of face-to-face.

I lent you my jumper to keep off the chill
and watched it standing back to behold
the butter bowl on the table in *Interior*

with *Woman at Piano, Strandgade 30,*
the light rendered as panes on the wall
in *Sunshine in the Drawing Room III,*

and the rulered lines of light
in our favourite,
Dust Motes Dancing in the Sunbeams.

III

Lost in the beauty of the subdued themes,
on getting round to the exit, I found you
waiting, smiling, my jumper over your left arm.

When we emerged the shop was in darkness,
the catalogue I'd promised myself
locked away, as so suddenly was my calm.

Anger, my jailor, strolled off whistling,
jangling his keys. He'd won.
In your unknowing world, near the street,

under the arch, I was a loaded gun.
I went off.
The courtyard pigeons erupted as one.

IV

I did not resound on Piccadilly.
I was talking; you heard me talk fiercely.
Talking and not shouting made it worse,

more personal, more cowardly—
what we had, whatever it was we had,
reduced to curses hissing off me.

You sat under the arch with your head
in your hands, dry-eyed and thinking, thinking.
When I was done, so were we.

V

I sat next to you, afraid to touch you,
apologising over and over,
blaming the faults of my father, his temper,

my *genes,* like a relapsed alcoholic.
You were thinking: how could you spend
your rare free days with someone like this?

How could you have—not *feelings,* as we
were one removed from that—a *fondness* for me,
who could be so tame one moment, then the next...?

Long black hair obscured your face,
but your body, making itself small, showed
the words, my unforgivable words, etched.

VI

I choked on my sorrys till silence.
Then you, over and over:
'God, Rob. God, Rob. God, Rob.'

A shake of the head, a sigh.
With a pride that made me want to love you
and cry, you moved off

like some fainted thing risen,
regaining strength with every stride,
and I followed you into the flow.

VII

I received a birthday present from you
when all this was months ago,
and we were, too.

Unwrapping it, I found the catalogue,
and inside you had written:
Dearest Rob, may you find your beauty
& inspiration within these pages…

Judy, I keep finding
they are not within those pages,
but in you, now and increasingly more.

LADY THATCHER

By the side door her van is parked
and bales lie side-by-side in the lane.
Was she here while I was showering,
lining yelm with her muff ligger?
Is it a good idea to call up
while she busies with her withy rod?

At elevenses, she comes down
for a builder's tea and a sandwich.
She stands against the ladder
scratching her gnat-bitten back,
stretching knees sore from the biddle,
braces unshouldered round her waist.

Seeing me in the window, she waves.
I wave back, pretend to be busy.
Maybe she'll catch her forefinger
with the spragger and need me
to carry out first aid, play doctor.
But she's done this hundreds of times.

Her fulfilment is no empty cliché
about 'A Woman in a Man's World',
it's something I inhabit, a warm dry
that keeps me snug in the backroom
when at my desk quoting Mao:
Women hold up half the sky.

OUTSIDE ELIZABETH ENDORFIELD'S

'Her attributes were distinctly Satanic; and those who looked no further called her, in plain terms, a witch. But she was not gaunt, nor ugly in the upper part of her face, nor particularly strange in manner...'
– Thomas Hardy, *Under the Greenwood Tree*

They see your chin and deem it pointed.
They see your russet cloak and deem it scarlet.
They never see you in their—our—church

and thus misjudge your intuition:
when the troubled come to you,
you sit them at your table as you pare potatoes

and the spell spun is by their own tongue;
their discord, aired, resolves
through no chant or tincture but your confidence.

I lack theirs, by which
I mean, they do not come to me. Nor I to you,
for I possess a tongue that your back to me,

a single purple hellebore in the bun
you wear your hair in as you scrape, scrape, scrape,
the splash as the potato finds its bucket,

each half-turn you make to the next
allowing a white flash of the literate jawline
that martyrs a man's sleep—

I possess a tongue that would be tied,
and by it you would know my distress.
So I watch you crochet by candlelight

from here, among the bat-triggered trees;
watch you bite your bottom lip in concentration,
a lure I resist: I shan't step forth, and halloo,

and chance you welcoming me in for tea,
for the moonlight could reveal my collar,
and you'd step back, your gaze grown cold.

No, Lizzy, I will not be so bold.
But tomorrow, tomorrow I will rail for you,
rail against petty tongues and superstitions

to their owners, that unbecoming lot,
and God can judge them if they should guess
whom I defend, and think us in scandal.

Forgive me, Lord, I would they were right!
It has grown cold. Bless you, Lizzy, bless you.
    Goodnight.

SHADOWS ON THE BARLEY

When our train goes over the river
sending all the bridge bats aquiver
into the pink evening;

when the poplar's shadow on the barley
is not wanting for company
and the castle turret is gleaming,

it's time for that part of the day,
a few hours at least, that we can say
are ours. The train slows down

into the freedom beyond the tunnel,
into the redbrick commuter town
where we can peel off our office flannel,

excited like kids home from school,
flinging windows wide, excitable
for the kettle's click, the shower,

for the can's nozzle in every flower;
then you, in your PJs already,
post-shower bob a glorious melee,

feet up on the kitchen table reading
the paper you didn't get to
on the morning train because, again,

we had slumped together in sleep,
in a jerking, dribbling heap,
dreaming of shadows on the barley.

III

Chevening

...we shall come home at last
To her sweet breast,
England's; by one touch be paid in full
For all things grey and long and terrible

– IVOR GURNEY

History is now and England

– T.S. ELIOT

I

Will you enter
          the maze with me?
                    Do you trust me to find the

way
          to the centre of things?
                    Do you

trust me to get us safely through
          without
                    needing directions

shouted
          from spectators on the bank,
                    or having to be

lifted and passed
          out like those toddler twins
                    to their mum

from daddy who's lost to his tether's end?
          These arms in these
                    rolled-up sleeves;

strong enough to hoist
          a child? Strong
                    enough to shield

the world from it,
          you,
                    us?

II

The train pulls you away from me,
our weekend in my country.
You speed through lavender and chalk
toward a London whose dusk
will echo to you treading Downs dust
and pollen into its pavements;

its tagged shutters and sick-flecked stops,
its scaffolding like the lies
propping up your peeling hopes
will make the cake stalls and book stalls
and little church on the Pilgrims' Way
feel more than thirty miles away.

From all you saw these past two days,
what will flash back to you neon-strong
after you've tossed your keys down,
opened your room up to yells and sirens,
no fresher air? Is it cruel of me
to hope you slump back in despair

because you see your place with eyes
rested from compromise?
It *is* cruel. You already miss somewhere
you're far from, farther than thirty miles:
home. But perhaps, one day maybe,
what you call that will be my own.

III

Your tread around the ornamental lake
  was comically unsure,
    your pumps picking with balletic care
     where to come down
      among the green goose shit.

We swayed, arm in arm,
  waited for the promised carp
    but saw only dull minnows
     in black lanes through green algae
      carved by a family of Greylag.

We stood before the purple door
  of an old wooden boathouse
    providing a moonlight-divined
     sanctum for illicit lovers
      or a murdered governess

scanning the water
  for her own reflection.
    We didn't enter,
     retracing our steps beneath
      the limes, the bubble-gum blossom.

IV

In the arboretum, under palms gifted
by diplomats at dim-distant summits
grown gaunt now with uncongenial climes,

you looked each way twice

then pressed me against the hot, red brick.
Your hair was slow through my fingers,
tasting salty, smelling of Ambre Solaire.

V

You made straight for the queue
snaking into a gazebo
where the right amount of coins

lifted the lid on a cool-box.
Sat on the lawn, it wasn't my book-finds
that made your eyes gleam,

or the 'Keyhole' cut through
the beeches on the distant Downs
giving us a mile of the future,

but the vanilla-cool that painted
a white petal on your chin.

VI

Through the graveyard filled with change-ringing,
in through the south door, hinges singing.
Powdery light from lancet windows
in the estate family's chantry
baptised you, the cobwebs unnerved;

enough light for the colonel (retd)
to take you all in, so when you transgressed—
running fingers along the white marble
and alabaster tombs—
he turned his good eye blind.

What did you expect your touch to find—
papier-mâché?
The tombs lie real as death's day,
rearing in all our futures,
except England's.

They died in childbirth and of the plague,
they died in their beds and on the veldt,
on Salient and Somme,
and here, as lit candles, live on.
At the door you leave a dollar donation.

VII

Your money bears the Queen's head but isn't sterling,
tender of a place where eyesight like a fish hawk's,
hearing like a timberwolf's, won't stop a man incurring
desolation's bite as he forays deeper, deeper north.

A place he went to wage his right to metal and hide,
where his scarlet tunic with gold-crown insignia
was a torch in the dusk of the uncontacted tribe,
a flare of remembrance on the thawing aiguille.

Then came a retreat back down the couloirs and trails
like blood draining from the head of a continent
for the boats to France, to advance with muddy details
on Vimy Ridge, and win the greatest monument:

a country, recognised, in statute and in spirit,
but with the Crown tipping the trading post's scales.
Dieppe; Juno; Holland. *Ut Incepit Fidelis Sic Permanet.*
Ottawa parks in June, awash with tulip petals.

VIII

The Queen's Own Royal West Kents

'Invicta' on their caps: undefeated—meaning England's
only people unconquered by the Norman invader,
reprised at Neuve Chapelle by the 1st Battalion
which stood firm, losing half its number.

Their four hundred names in stone west of the Medway
do not change in towns they would half-recognise.
Enterprise centres stand where they mowed their hay,
new homes oust the shade they took bait in, at ease.

Still horses though: the white stallion breeze-rampant
in his red field, flying from obscure prefabs by the railway line,
council offices, and from other points less permanent:
Cricket Week marquee, pop-up library. Divine

is the sun's countenance on the august wheat,
on the cut lavender, the flags, the fallen's roundabout.
They live. Back lanes are dusted by their returning feet,
murmur to the bawdy songs of their mustering out.

They move into the field-sweet air; the women turn
from sheaving, rush disbelieving to their dearest ones
who kiss them, lead them into the shade, the fern.
Their names our fathers bore, then us; now our sons.

IX

Gavelkind

Undefeated, it survived that a Kent man's intestacy
    left all his sons equally a gentleman.
No primogeniture: an equality
    on earth, as it is in heaven.

Womenfolk too, if they could speak
    in straw-floored court their blood-cord to the dead,
received a share with which to sow and reap
    their daily bread.

No confiscation by the Crown
    of the inheritance of those who trespassed.
Any attempt brought across the Down
    men with halberds interlocked so none might pass.

'You did not need deliverance,'
    the faces in the rood screens and stained glass say,
'from what was your inheritance:
    are things any better in your day?'

Standing in their nave to their prayer,
    sheltered from all temporal pressure,
I feel on the back of my neck the hard stare
    of their power and glory, forever.

X

This is the real England, I say, so what do you think?
It's a place of trees; of apple, pear, cherry and plum.
In the gaps is man's history, his urge to link
with others, forge commerce, lick a thumb
to count the realm's tender or sample harvest.
The railway came, but the speed it gave the world
entangled in this bracken and broomy darkness.
Life here is at the pace a picnic blanket unfurls.
Do you want to reset your watch to the toll of here?
Our years would lengthen into a summer's evening
of wine on a lawn under bat flight. Then we'll disappear.
All that'll be left: two glasses filled with morning,
your silk scarf over one of the two empty chairs;
two lit candles in the church for us, if anyone cares.

XI

I lie in the strangeness of after you being here,
quilted in your perfume, lit by your message,
happy not feeling relieved I'm alone again.

I flick through the books—all-you-can-carry-for-50p—
releasing the scent of privet-screened studies
where restraint only relaxes in florid hand

on a flyleaf: *To Anne, with all my love;*
Hugh, with love. We think it's funny—and really hope
that you will too! From Meg, Xmas 1938.

Looking closely, long strands of your Han-black hair
lie all around the bed, not just on your side.
It's everywhere, sticking to my tread,

and when I step on a certain part of the floor
the kiwi bird toy you couldn't resist winding up—
even knowing an ex had bought it for me—

jolts into life, cloth beak butting the bookshelf
while, for some reason, as it has always done,
it hops along backward, bumping

into your own offering you left there:
a keyring cuddly toy moose in Mountie uniform.
He stares back beadily from under his brim

as I consider how big my pocket needs to be
to accommodate him. With sunlight still
on the chalk escarpment, on Star Hill Wood,

but draining from here like cows down the lane,
I have received word you're home safe.
A freshness elates the darkening trees.

XII

England did all it could. It hoisted the brolly
of its microclimate and put on its best southern face;
it drew back the nettles and oil-painted
its moths into butterflies. It muted the motorway
but turned up the wood pigeons' volume,
darted the walks with proud robin.

It lowered the ceiling of the shade, cosily,
and healed the woodworm in the beams.
Each interior, from the road, was a castle
from a yeoman's dreams: a hearth,
a table at which to break the won bread,
an armchair, bookcase and a lamp; upstairs,
beyond net curtains, a white pillow for his head.

When he comes to rest his head on another,
a distance from here, conveyed to it shrilly
through traffic under a flag of truce,
he will think of his castle and realise what he
inherited will be inherited from him soon,
and find peace in that, as the boatman takes his fee
glinting in the light of a bomber's moon.

Yes, England did all it could.
All of it becomes propaganda with an airmail stamp.
All of it evocable at a whiff of buddleia.
It wreathed the dead, straightened the steeple,
placed the fielders, re-glazed the red phone box.
Now I must wait for the needle
of your heart's compass to unspin,
and see where it stops.